MUCHAS Palabras Sobre MI CASA

MUCHAS Palabras Sobre MI CASA

Ilustrado por Richard Brown

HBJ

A Voyager/HBJ Book

Harcourt Brace Jovanovich, Publishers

San Diego   New York   London

Requests for permission to make copies of any
part of the work should be mailed to: Copyrights and
Permissions Department, Harcourt Brace Jovanovich, Publishers,
Orlando, Florida 32887.

Translation by Claudia Owen

100 words about my house. Spanish.
   Muchas palabras sobre mi casa/ilustrado por Richard Brown.
      p. cm.
   Translation of: 100 words about my house.
   "A Voyager/HBJ book."
   Summary: Labeled illustrations depict items found around the
house.
   ISBN 0-15-200532-3
   1. House furnishings — Terminology — Juvenile literature. 2. House
furnishings — Pictorial works — Juvenile literature. 3. Picture
dictionaries. Spanish — Juvenile literature. [1. House furnishings —
Pictorial works. 2. Vocabulary. 3. Spanish language materials.]
I. Brown, Richard Eric, 1946-   ill. II. Title. III. Title: Mi
casa.
TX311.A1518 1989   88-21363
645′.03′61 — dc19

Printed in Singapore

First edition

A B C D E

Para Al y Keith
—R. B.

chimenea
chimney

césped
lawn

buzón
mailbox

baúl de juguetes
toy chest

camilla de niño
bassinet

cuna
crib

lamparilla
night-light

corralito
playpen

EN EL CUARTO DE MI HERMANO

IN MY BROTHER'S ROOM

clóset

closet

cama litera

bunk bed

EN EL CUARTO DE MI HERMANA

IN MY SISTER'S ROOM

dosel

canopy

colcha

quilt

afiche
poster

globo terrestre
globe

cómoda
dresser

EN EL CUARTO DE MIS PADRES

IN MY PARENT'S ROOM

tocador

vanity

estante para libros

bookcase

cama

bed

fotografía

picture

televisor

television

reloj
clock

mesa de noche
nightstand

alacena
cupboard

radio
radio

tarro de galletas
cookie jar

lavaplatos
dishwasher

toalla
towel

ducha
shower

bañera
bathtub

cesto
hamper

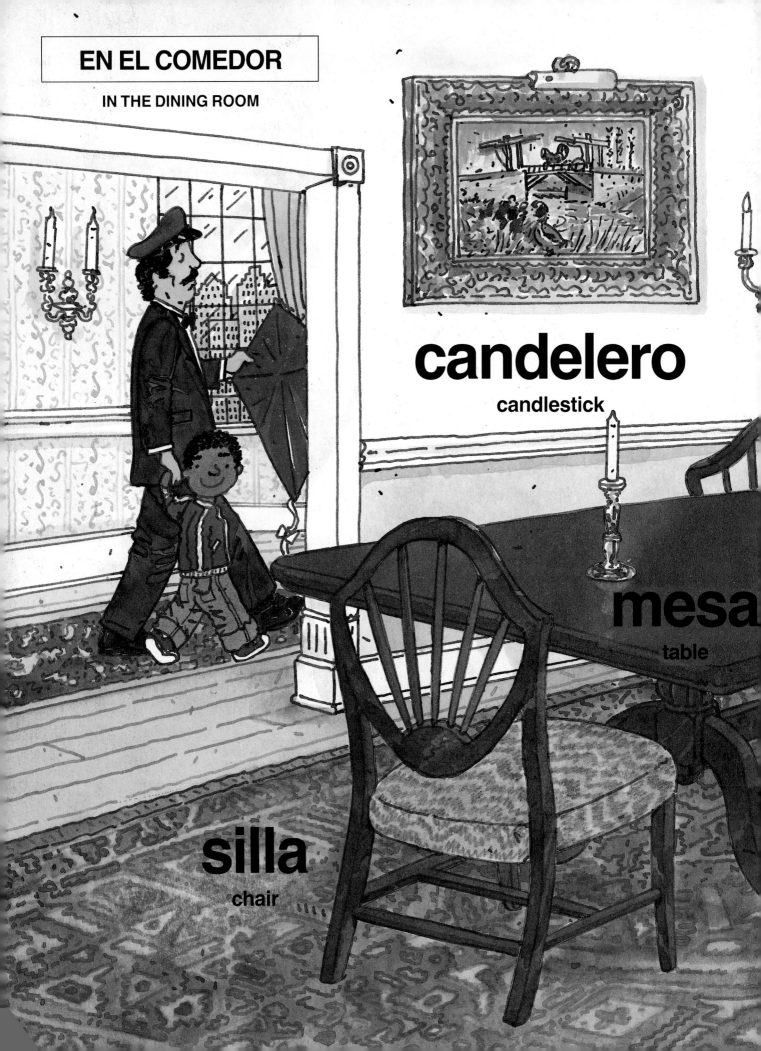

candelero

candlestick

mesa

table

silla

chair

araña de luces
chandelier

aparador
sideboard

silla alta
high chair

alfombra
rug

cuadro
painting

manto
mantel

chimenea
fireplace

piano
piano

plancha

iron

mesa de planchar

ironing board

aspiradora

vacuum

lavadora
washing machine

secadora
dryer

mecedora

rocking chair

fonógrafo

phonograph

baúl

trunk

linterna
lantern

coche cuna
carriage

caja
box

automóvil

car

caja de herramientas

toolbox

escalera
ladder

mesa de trabajo
worktable

bicicleta
bicycle

EN EL JARDIN DE ATRAS

IN THE BACKYARD

columpios
swing set

casita de juguete
playhouse

cerca
fence

huerto
garden

patio

patio

barbacoa

barbeque